MW00993468

Fabulous Feedsack Quilts

by The Editors of *Traditional Quiltworks* magazine

A PATTERN BOOK

CHITRA PUBLICATIONS

Your Best Value in Quilting!

Copyright © 1999 by Chitra Publications

All Rights Reserved. Published in the United States of America.

Printed in Hong Kong.

Chitra Publications

2 Public Avenue

Montrose, Pennsylvania 18801

No part of this publication may be reproduced or transmitted in any form or by any means, electronic or mechanical, including photocopy, recording, or any information storage and retrieval system now known or to be invented, without permission in writing from the publisher, except by a reviewer who wishes to quote brief passages in connection with a review written for inclusion in a magazine, newspaper, or broadcast.

First printing: 1999

Library of Congress Cataloging-in-Publication Data

Fabulous feedsack quilts : a pattern book / by the editors of Traditional quiltworks magazine.

    p.   cm.

  ISBN 1-885588-25-9

  1. Patchwork—Patterns.   2. Patchwork quilts.   3. Bagging.

  I. Traditional quiltworks.

  TT835.F315 1999

746.46′041—dc21   98-52901

                                         CIP

Editors: The editors of *Traditional Quiltworks* magazine

Design and Illustrations: Kimberly Grace

Cover and Inside Photography: Van Zandbergen Photography, Brackney, PA

Our Mission Statement

We publish quality quilting magazines and books that recognize, promote and inspire self-expression. We are dedicated to serving our customers with respect, kindness and efficiency.

Oh, those fabulous feedsacks! Not only are they popular collectibles, but when used in quilts they also add vibrancy and a touch of nostalgia to your home. There are so many feedsack enthusiasts who are also quilters that they have banded together in an international organization known as The Feedsack Club. Members swap feedsacks and charm squares cut from them, avidly share feedsack lore with each other and attend regional gatherings devoted to their interest. Several club members share their lovely full-size feedsack quilts with you in this book and we offer a pattern for each of them along with several others.

What is the story behind our fascination with this part of Americana? Feedsacks were originally utilitarian cloth bags used for packaging such items as seed, flour, sugar, grain and animal feed. Frugal farm folks recycled the cloth bags into useful household items such as curtains, dish towels, quilts and clothing. First made from burlap or plain white cotton printed with company logos, feedsacks ultimately evolved into a useful marketing tool. Companies that recognized the appeal of feedsacks to homemakers of the early 20th century began to make them from dyed solid cottons and colorful prints—florals, geometrics, plaids, polka dots and novelty designs. They often included instructions for removing the logo from a bag to extend the use of fabric and used a chain stitch closure which was easy to remove without damaging the cloth.

While the use of feedsacks for packaging declined by the mid-20th century, textile lovers have continued to collect and preserve these pieces of American textile history as well as the quilts made from them. Quiltmaker Lynette Crawford, whose "Snails Trail" quilt is featured in this book, recalls, "When I was a child living on a farm, my mother bought feed for her chickens in colorful cotton sacks. She then made our dresses, sheets, cup towels and underwear from the empty sacks."

Perhaps Lynette's recollections best reflect the nostalgic "tug" we feel upon seeing a feedsack quilt. Capture the feeling when you make your quilts using the patterns in this book. Use vintage scraps, reproduction prints or fabrics of your choice. We offer a variety of construction techniques for all skill levels, including several no-template patterns. Two of the quilts have prairie point edgings—one with a novel pieced variety. The Straight Furrows Log Cabin gives you a choice of traditional piecing or a quick "quilt-as-you-sew" method. No matter which quilt you choose to make first, we wish you many happy hours of stitching!

The Editors of Traditional Quiltworks magazine

Table of Contents

Pattern Ratings
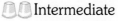 Beginner   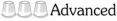 Intermediate   Advanced

Drunkard's Path

Try your hand at curves in this "devilish" version of a favorite.

QUILT SIZE: 97" x 105"
BLOCK SIZE: 4" square

MATERIALS

Yardage is estimated for 44" fabric.

- Assorted print scraps totaling at least 7 yards
- 7 3/4 yards white
- 9 yards backing fabric
- 101" x 109" piece of batting

CUTTING

Pattern pieces are full size and include a 1/4" seam allowance.

- Cut 224: A, assorted prints
- Cut 304: B, assorted prints
- Cut 96: D, assorted prints
- Cut 4: E, assorted prints
- Cut 304: A, white
- Cut 224: B, white
- Cut 92: C, white
- Cut 1: 36" square, white; then cut 2 1/2"-wide bias strips from it and join them to make a long binding strip.

PIECING

- Sew a print A to a white B to make a Drunkard's Path block, easing the curved edges to fit. Make 224.

- In the same manner, sew a white A to a print B. Make 304.
- Lay out 16 blocks with print A's and 20 with print B's, as shown. Sew them into rows and join the rows to make a Big Block. Make 8.

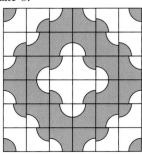

- Sew the Big Blocks into 2 vertical rows of 4. Join the rows to make the center row.
- Lay out 12 blocks with print A's and 18 with print B's as shown. Sew them into rows and join the rows for a partial Big Block. Make 8.

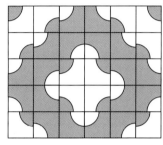

- Sew the partial Big Blocks into 2 vertical rows of 4, to make the outside rows.
- Referring to the quilt photo as needed, lay out these 2 rows on opposite sides of the center row. Join the rows.
- Sew a print D to a white C to make a pieced unit, as shown. Make 88.

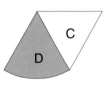

- Sew 23 pieced units into a row. Stitch a white C to the print D at the end of the row, to make a long pieced border. Make 2.
- In the same manner, sew 21 pieced units into a row, stitching a white C to the print D at the end of the row to make a short pieced border. Make 2.
- Stitch the long pieced borders to opposite sides of the quilt, starting, stopping and backstitching 1/4" from the raw edges.
- Sew a print E between 2 print D's, as shown, to make a pieced corner. Make 4.

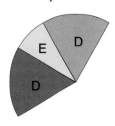

- Sew a pieced corner to each end of the 2 short pieced borders.
- Stitch these to the remaining sides of the quilt.
- Finish the quilt as described in *To Make a Quilt* using the long white bias binding strip.

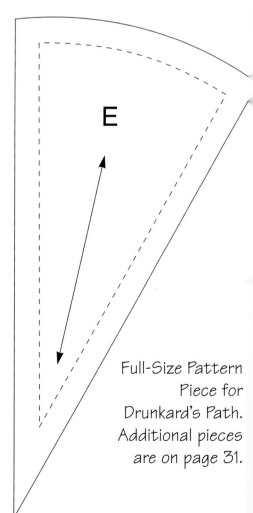

Full-Size Pattern Piece for Drunkard's Path. Additional pieces are on page 31.

Charlene Brewer, of Bethany, Oklahoma, reversed the placement of dark and light blocks in her "Drunkard's Path" quilts (each 97" x 105") to produce mirror images. Charlene titled the quilts **"Alternative Reflections I"** *(right) and* **"Alternative Reflections II."** *(bottom) (patterned on opposite page). This layout of Drunkard's Path blocks is known as Devil's Puzzle.*

Dream of Blue Roses

Try your hand at curved piecing.

QUILT SIZE: 61" x 73"
BLOCK SIZE: 6"

MATERIALS
Yardage is estimated for 44" fabric.
• Assorted blue print scraps totaling at least 2 1/4 yards
• 4 1/2 yards muslin
• 4 1/2 yards backing fabric
• 65" x 77" piece of batting

CUTTING
Dimensions include a 1/4" seam allowance.
NOTE: *Cut the lengthwise muslin border strips first, before cutting the smaller pieces from that fabric.*
For each of the 40 dark blocks:
• Cut 2: 2" squares, muslin
• Cut 2: A, blue print
• Cut 1: B, muslin
For each of the 40 light blocks:
• Cut 2: 2" squares, blue print
• Cut 2: A, muslin
• Cut 1: B, same blue print
Also:
• Cut 4: 6 1/2" x 64" strips, muslin, for the border
• Cut 7: 2 1/2" x 44" strips, muslin, for the binding

PIECING
• Pin and sew a blue print A to a muslin B, start and stop 1/4" from the ends and backstitch. Clip the seam allowance along the curve and press toward the A. Set aside.

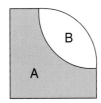

• Sew 2" muslin squares to each short side of a matching blue print A, as shown.

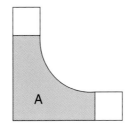

• Pin and sew the two units together to make a dark block. Clip the seam allowance along the curve and press toward the A. Make 40.

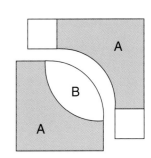

• In the same manner, but reversing the colors and pressing toward the dark B's,

Full-Size Pattern Pieces for Dream of Blue Roses

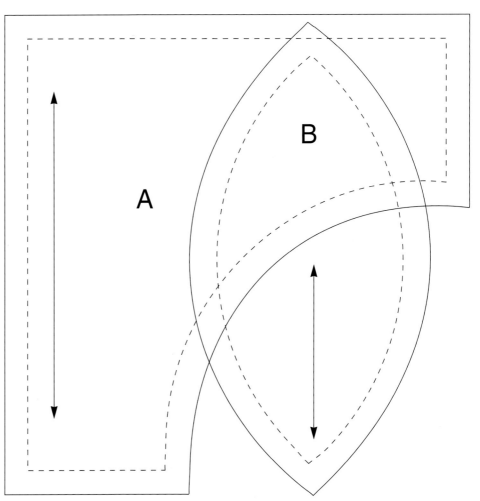

▶ *Using a pattern that was popular in the 1930s, Patricia Reid of Titusville, Florida, collected 42 feedsack prints for* **"Dream of the Blue Roses"** *(60" x 72"). The entire quilt is composed of the same pattern that has been flipped-flopped in alternating blocks. Notice how the muslin and feedsack prints also alternate between each block, creating a dynamic contrast with positive and negative space.*

make 40 light blocks, as shown.

• Lay out two light blocks and two dark blocks, alternating their positions. Make sure the B's radiate from the center, as shown. Pin and sew the blocks together in pairs. Join the pairs to make a large block.

Make 20.

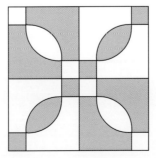

• Lay the large blocks out in five rows of four, referring to the photo as needed. Sew the blocks into rows and join the rows.

• Measure the length of the quilt. Trim 2 of the 6 1/2" x 64" muslin strips to that measurement and sew them to the sides of the quilt.

• Measure the width of the quilt including the borders. Trim the remaining 6 1/2" x 64" strips to that measurement and sew them to the top and bottom of the quilt.

• Finish the quilt as described in *To Make a Quilt*, using the 2 1/2" x 44" muslin strips for binding.

Axe Blade Charm Quilt

Show off your collection of prints in this classic one-patch quilt.

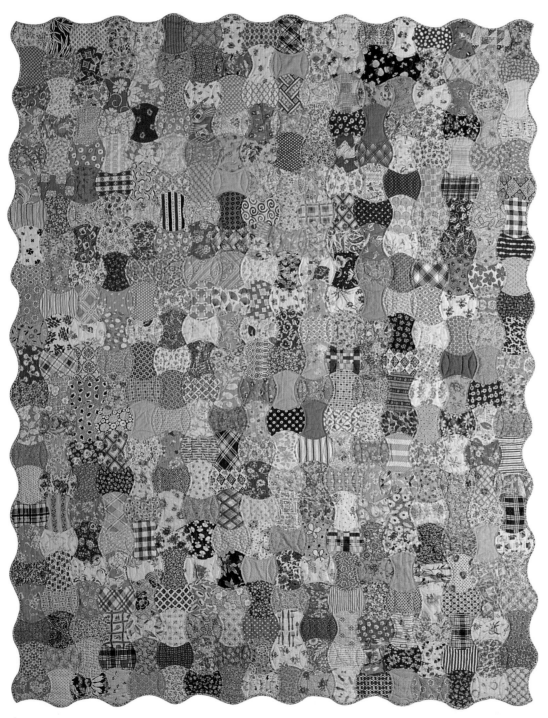

QUILT SIZE: 83" x 106"

MATERIALS
Yardage is estimated for 44" fabric.
• Assorted scraps totaling at least 9 1/2 yards
NOTE: *Include a variety of color values ranging from light to dark.*
• 1 yard light blue print for the binding
• 6 1/2 yards backing fabric
• 87" x 110" piece of batting

CUTTING
The pattern piece is full size and includes a 1/4" seam allowance.
• Cut 414: A, assorted prints
• Cut 1: 36" square, light blue print; then cut 2 1/2"-wide bias strips from it and join them to make a long binding strip.

PIECING
• Sew the A's together in pairs, as shown, easing the curved edges to fit.

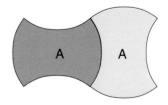

• Sew 9 pairs into a row. Make 23 rows.
• Join the rows, referring to the photo as needed.
• Finish the quilt as described in *To Make a Quilt* using the light blue print binding strip.

▲ *Charlene Brewer purchased a small quilt top which she enlarged to make* **"Axe Blade Charm Quilt"** *(83" x 106"). She replaced duplicate pieces in the original quilt top and any that were not cut from feedsack fabrics. The quilt is composed of more than 400 different prints. Charlene notes that two dark blue pieces are the same color and design, but their weaves differ. Can you find them?*

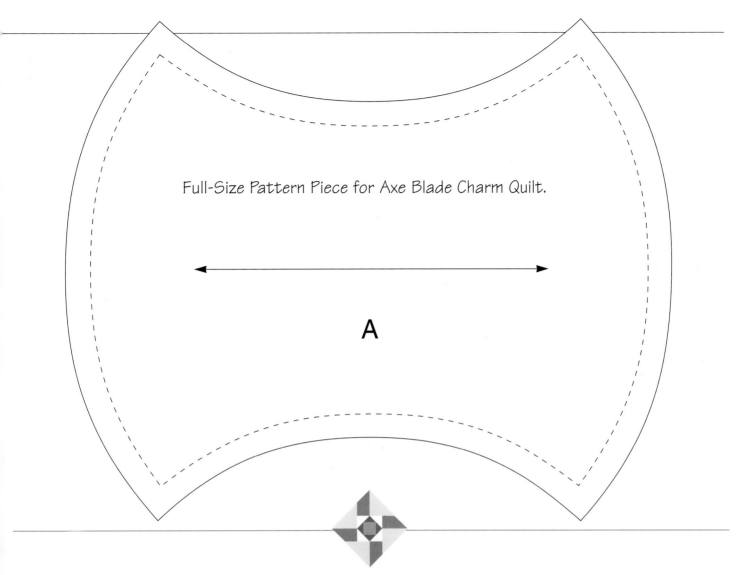

Full-Size Pattern Piece for Axe Blade Charm Quilt.

A

Feedsack Shooting Star

Partial seams make sewing these blocks a breeze!

Shown on page 10
QUILT SIZE: 85" square
BLOCKS SIZE: 12"

MATERIALS
Yardage is estimated for 44" fabric.
• 3 1/2 yards muslin
• Assorted feedsack or other print scraps totaling at least 5 1/2 yards.
NOTE: *Sizes should range from 3" x 3" to 3 1/2" x 7".*
• 49 yellow solid and blue solid scraps each at least 4" x 8"
• 3/4 yard dark print for the binding
• 5 yards backing fabric
• 89" square piece of batting

CUTTING

Dimensions include a 1/4" seam allowance.
• Cut 49: 9" squares, muslin; then cut each in quarters diagonally to yield 196 triangles
• Cut 49: 3 1/2" squares, assorted prints
NOTE: *These are the centers of the blocks. You may want to cut them individually to highlight a motif in each fabric.*
• Cut 2: 3" squares, from each of 49 prints; then cut each in half diagonally to yield 196 small triangles.
• Cut 2: 3 7/8" squares, from each of 49 different yellow or blue solids; then cut each in half diagonally to yield 196 medium triangles.
• Cut 4: 3 1/2" x 6 3/8" rectangles, from each of 49 different prints. Group them in matching sets of 4.
• Cut 9: 2 1/2" x 44" strips, dark print for

the binding
PIECING
• Sew a 3 1/2" x 6 3/8" print rectangle to each of the muslin triangles, as shown. Be sure to sew the rectangle to the same side of each triangle. Set aside these pieced muslin units in matching sets of four.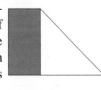
• Take these pieces for a block center: a 3 1/2" print square, 4 matching small print triangles, and 4 matching medium solid triangles. Center and sew 2 small print triangles to opposite sides of the 3 1/2" print square. Press the seam allowances toward the triangles. Sew the other 2 small print triangles to the remaining sides of the

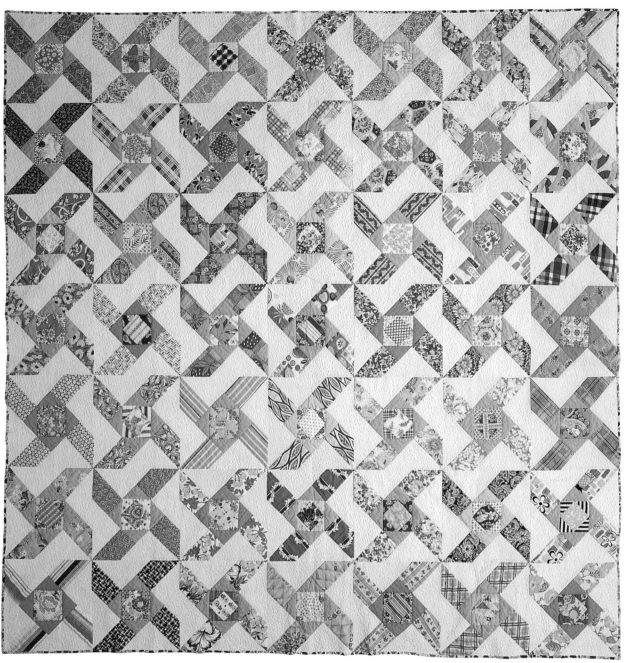

*◀ Ellie Hudacsek of Ambridge, Pennsylvania, used vintage scraps to make her **"Feedsack Shooting Star"** (85" square). A self-taught quilter, she was inspired by a pattern in Sara Nephew's book,* Designs from the Thirties. *Despite Ellie's preference for traditional patterns, she makes the most of modern methods, like the machine quilting that highlights this antique design.*

square. Press seam allowances toward the triangles.

• Center and sew 2 medium solid triangles to opposite sides of the unit. Press the seam allowances toward the triangles. Sew the other two medium triangles to the remaining sides to make a center unit. Press as before.

• Make 49 center units. Group each one with four matching pieced muslin units.

• Referring to the diagram, pin one of the pieced muslin units to a center unit. Sew a partial seam, starting at the corner of the rectangle and ending just past the seam with the muslin triangle. Do not sew to the end of the center unit. Backstitch and

remove any pins so that the remainder of the muslin triangle is not attached to the center unit.

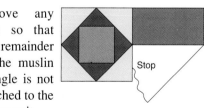

• Working counter-clockwise, pin another pieced muslin unit to the center unit and sew a full seam to the end of the muslin triangle. Repeat with the third and fourth pieced muslin units.

• Pin the remainder of the first muslin triangle to the last muslin unit and complete the seam.

• Press the block. Trim to 12 1/2" square,

cutting off the excess from the 3 1/2" x 6 3/8" rectangles.

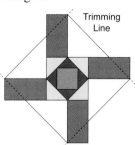

Trimming Line

• Lay out the blocks in 7 rows of 7. Sew the blocks into rows and join the rows.

• Finish the quilt as described in *To Make a Quilt*, using the 2 1/2" x 44" dark print strips for binding.

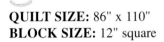

Jacob's Ladder

Piece your own ladder to success with cheerful prints and stripes.

QUILT SIZE: 86" x 110"
BLOCK SIZE: 12" square

MATERIALS

*Yardage is estimated for 44"
fabric.*
• Assorted prints totaling at
least 4 yards
NOTE: *In the pictured quilt,
most of the prints contain at
least some yellow.*
• 4 yards white
• 3 1/4 yards yellow stripe
• 7 3/4 yards backing fabric
• 90" x 114" piece of batting

CUTTING

*Dimensions include a 1/4"
seam allowance.*
For each of 48 blocks:
• Cut 1: 2 1/2" x 26" strip,
print
• Cut 2: 4 7/8" squares,
same print
• Cut 1: 2 1/2" x 26" strip,
white
• Cut 2: 4 7/8" squares,
white
Also:
• Cut 2: 7" x 114" lengthwise strips, yellow stripe, for
the border

(Continued on the following page)

▶ *Quilting teacher Connie
Tilman of Powhatan, Virginia,
pieced this **"Jacob's Ladder"**
(86" x 110"). Most of the prints
in her quilt contain at least
some yellow to coordinate with
the striped border. She's been
collecting feedsacks and other
vintage textiles since 1990.*

- Cut 2: 7" x 90" lengthwise strips, yellow stripe, for the border
- Cut 4: 2 1/2" x 114" lengthwise strips, yellow stripe, for the binding

PIECING

- Sew a 2 1/2" print strip to a 2 1/2" white strip along their length to make a pieced strip. Press the seam allowance toward the print. Cut ten 2 1/2" slices from the pieced strip.
- Sew 2 slices into a Four Patch. Make 5. Set them aside.
- Draw a diagonal line from corner to corner on the wrong side of each 4 7/8" white square.
- Lay a marked white square on a 4 7/8" print square, right sides together. Sew 1/4" away from the diagonal line on both sides. Cut the squares apart on the marked line to yield 4 pieced squares. Open them and press the seam allowance toward the print.
- Sew Four Patches to opposite sides of a pieced square to make a row, as shown. Make 2.

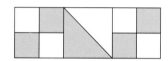

- Sew pieced squares to opposite sides of the remaining Four Patch to make a center row, as shown.

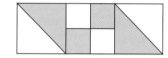

- Sew the three rows together to form a Jacob's Ladder block. Make 48.

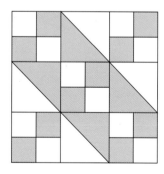

- Lay out the blocks in 8 rows of 6. Sew the blocks into rows and join the rows.
- Center and sew the 7" x 114" yellow stripe strips to the sides of the quilt top, starting and stopping 1/4" from the raw edges.
- Center and sew the 7" x 90" yellow stripe strips to the top and bottom of the quilt in the same manner. Miter each corner, referring to the mitering section in *To Make a Quilt*, as needed.
- Finish the quilt as described in *To Make a Quilt*, using the 2 1/2" x 114" yellow stripe strips for binding.

Snails Trail

Get a fast start by rotary cutting pieces for this quilt.

QUILT SIZE: 76" x 80"
BLOCK SIZE: 12" square

MATERIALS

Yardage is estimated for 44" fabric.
- Assorted scraps totaling 3 1/4 yards
- 2 1/4 yards muslin
- 3/4 yard dark print for the binding
- 5 yards backing fabric
- 80" x 84" piece of batting

CUTTING

All dimensions include a 1/4" seam allowance.
- Cut 36: 6 7/8" squares, assorted prints; then cut each in half diagonally to yield 72 large triangles
- Cut 36: 5 1/8" squares, assorted prints; then cut each in half diagonally to yield 72 medium triangles
- Cut 36: 3 7/8" squares, assorted prints; then cut each in half diagonally to yield 72 small triangles
- Cut 36: 3" squares assorted prints; then cut each in half diagonally to yield 72 tiny triangles
- Cut 72: 2" squares, assorted prints
- Cut 24: 4 1/4" x 6 1/2" strips, assorted prints, for the top and bottom borders
- Cut 24: 2" x 6 1/2" strips, assorted prints, for the side borders
- Cut 4: 2" x 4 1/4" strips, assorted prints, for the side borders
- Cut 8: 2 1/2" x 44" strips, dark print, for the binding
- Cut 36: 6 7/8" squares, muslin; then cut each in half diagonally to yield 72 large triangles
- Cut 36: 5 1/8" squares, muslin; then cut each in half diagonally to yield 72 medium triangles
- Cut 36: 3 7/8" squares, muslin; then cut each in half diagonally to yield 72 small triangles
- Cut 36: 3" squares, muslin; then cut each in half diagonally to yield 72 tiny triangles
- Cut 72: 2" squares, muslin

DIRECTIONS

For each of the 36 Snails Trail blocks:
- Lay out two 2" print squares and two 2" muslin squares, as shown. Sew them together into a Four Patch.

- Sew two tiny print triangles to opposite sides of the Four Patch. Sew a tiny muslin triangle to

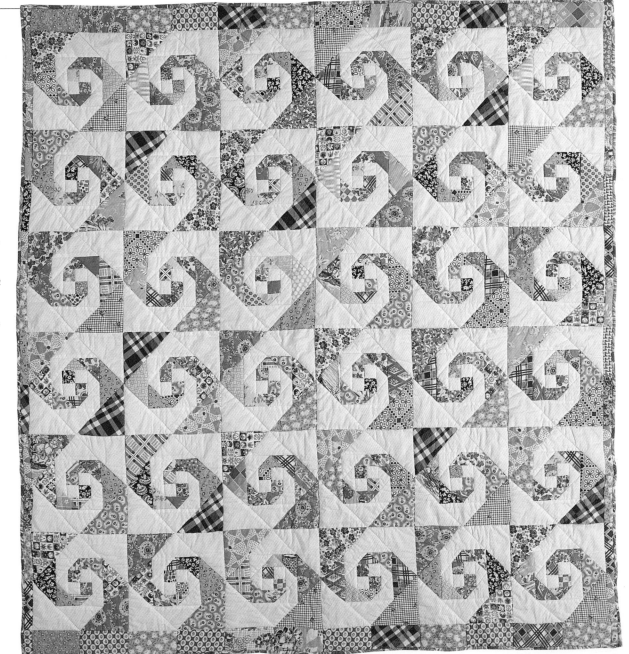

▶ *Lynette Crawford of Belton, Texas, pieced this "Snails Trail" (76" x 80") quilt, an old-fashioned design. She enjoys exchanging 6" feed-sack squares with others. Lynette has fond memories of living on a farm and seeing her mother use feed-sacks for dresses, sheets and towels.*

each remaining side of the Four Patch, as shown.

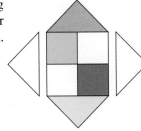

• Noting the placement of this pieced square, sew small print triangles to the upper right and lower left sides of the square. Sew small muslin triangles to the upper left and lower right sides of the square, as shown.

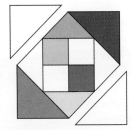

• Sew medium print triangles to the right and left sides of this pieced square. Sew medium muslin triangles to the top and bottom of the square, as shown.

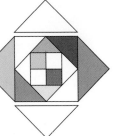

• Sew large print triangles to the upper left and lower right sides of this square. Sew large muslin triangles to the upper right and lower left sides of the square to complete a block, as shown.

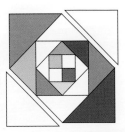

• Lay out the blocks in 6 rows of 6. Sew the blocks into rows and join the rows.

• Piece the top border by sewing 12 of the 4 1/4" x 6 1/2" print strips together end to end. Using the remaining 12 strips, piece the bottom border in the same manner. Sew the borders to the quilt.

• Piece a side border by sewing 12 of the 2" x 6 1/2" print strips together end to end. Make 2. Sew a 2" x 4 1/4" print strip to each end of each side border. Sew these borders to the quilt.

• Finish the quilt as described in *To Make a Quilt*, using the 2 1/2" x 44" dark print strips for binding.

13

Rose Star

Just perfect for scraps!

QUILT SIZE: 86" x 96"
BLOCK SIZE: 18" x 20"

MATERIALS
Yardage is estimated for 44" fabric.
- Solid color scraps totaling about 1 yard
- Print scraps totaling about 5 1/2 yards
- 1 1/8 yards blue solid
- 5 yards white
- 7/8 yard fabric for the binding
- 8 1/2 yards backing fabric
- 90" x 100" piece of batting

CUTTING
Pattern pieces are full size and include a 1/4" seam allowance, as do all dimensions given. We recommend making a sample block before cutting fabric for the whole quilt. Cut the white strips parallel to the selvage before cutting other pieces from that fabric.
- Cut 4: 3 1/2" x 92" lengthwise strips, white
- Cut 660: A, white
- Cut 170: A, blue solid
- Cut 9: 2 1/2" x 44" strips, fabric for the binding
For each of 23 whole blocks:
- Cut 6: A, solid color
- Cut 12: A, first print
- Cut 12: A, second print
- Cut 12: A, third print
For each of 4 half-blocks:
- Cut 3: A, solid color
- Cut 6: A, first print
- Cut 6: A, second print
- Cut 6: A, third print
For each of 8 side units:
- Cut 2: A, first print
- Cut 1: B and BR, second print
- Cut 1: B and BR, white
For each of 2 corner units:
- Cut 1: A, first print
- Cut 1: BR, second print
- Cut 1: B, white
For each of 2 reverse corner units:
- Cut 1: A, first print

- Cut 1: B, second print
- Cut 1: BR, white

PIECING
- Take the pieces you cut for a single block, along with 6 blue solid A's and 24 white A's. Lay out the block as indicated—start with the 6 solid color scrap A's in the center, surrounded by 12 print A's. The blue solid A's become the points of the star, while the white A's form the outer edge. Make sure you are satisfied with the arrangement of colors and the contrast before you start stitching.

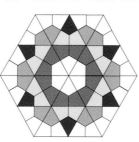

- This block is fairly simple to piece if you think in terms of triangles. Join A's in 3's to make small pieced triangles. Then join the small pieced triangles in 4's to make large pieced triangles.
- Join the large pieced triangles in 3's to make half-blocks. For the present, don't join the halves—but pin them together so the corresponding halves don't go astray. Make 23 Rose Star blocks in this way.

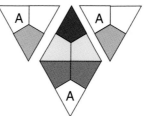

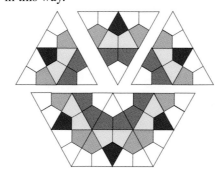

- Take the scrap pieces you cut for a half-block, along with 3 blue solid A's and 12 white A's. Construct the half-block just as you did the whole blocks. Make 4.
- Take the pieces you cut for a side unit, along with 2 blue solid A's and 6 white A's. Lay them out as indicated to check the balance of colors and contrast.

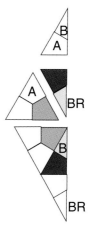

- Stitch the pieces into triangles, then join the triangles. Make 8 side units.

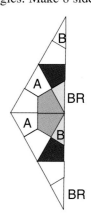

- Take the pieces for a corner and reverse corner unit, along with 1 blue solid A and 3 white A's for each. Construct the corner units as you did the side units. Make 2 of each type.

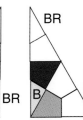

Make 2   Make 2

▶ *Think "triangles" when you piece this intricate "**Rose Star Quilt**" (86" x 96"). Anna Wescott of Logansport, Indiana, chose this old-time pattern to show off her growing collection of colorful feedsack fabrics. The blue star points in each block lend continuity to the design, while the white furnishes a quiet background for the many busy prints.*

ASSEMBLY

• Lay out the blocks, half-blocks, side units and corner units referring to the photo. Stitch the units into rows, then join the rows.

• Measure the length of the quilt. Trim two of the 3 1/2" x 92" white strips to equal this measurement. Sew them to opposite sides of the quilt.

• Measure the width of the quilt, including the borders. Trim the remaining 3 1/2" x 92" white strips to equal this measurement. Sew them to the remaining sides of the quilt.

• Finish the quilt as described in *To Make a Quilt*. Using the 2 1/2" x 44" fabric strips for binding.

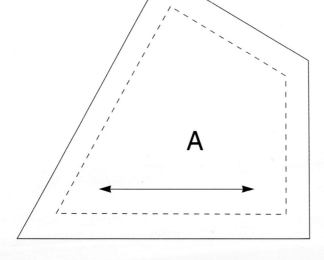

A

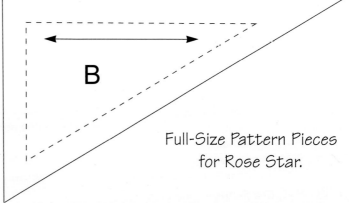

B

Full-Size Pattern Pieces for Rose Star.

Straight Furrows

Stitch a lively Log Cabin the traditional way or quilt it as you sew.

QUILT SIZE: 85" x 99"
BLOCK SIZE: 14"

MATERIALS
Yardage is estimated for 44" fabric.
• 1 yard red print for block centers and binding
• Assorted light print scraps totaling at least 3 3/4 yards
• Assorted dark print scraps totaling at least 4 3/4 yards
• 6 yards backing fabric
• 89" x 103" piece of batting

CUTTING
Dimensions include a 1/4" seam allowance. The quilter used 3 light fabrics and 3 dark fabrics for each block.
To create the zig-zag effect, in each diagonal row, the quilter used the same dark fabric and the same light fabric for the last positions in each block.
• Cut 42: 2 1/2" squares, red print
• Cut 42: 2 1/2" squares, assorted light prints
• Cut 84: 2 1/2" x 4 1/2" strips, half from light prints and half from dark prints
• Cut 84: 2 1/2" x 6 1/2" strips, half from light prints and half from dark prints
• Cut 84: 2 1/2" x 8 1/2" strips, half from light prints and half from dark prints
• Cut 84: 2 1/2" x 10 1/2" strips, half from light prints and half from dark prints
• Cut 84: 2 1/2" x 12 1/2" strips, half from light prints and half from dark prints
• Cut 42: 2 1/2" x 14 1/2" strips, dark prints
• Cut 9: 2 1/2" x 44" strips, red print, for binding

PIECING
• Stitch a 2 1/2" light print square to each 2 1/2" red square for the center units, chain sewing them. Clip the units apart and press seam allowances away from the red square.
• Stitch a 2 1/2" x 4 1/2" light print strip

to each center unit, as shown. Clip the units apart and press away from the center unit.

• Stitch a 2 1/2" x 4 1/2" dark print strip to each unit, as shown. Clip and press as before.

• Stitch a 2 1/2" x 6 1/2" dark print strip to each unit, as shown. Clip and press as before.

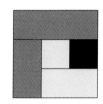

• Continue in the same manner, stitching appropriate length strips to each unit in a clockwise direction and alternating two light strips, then two dark strips. Be sure one half of the block is light and the other half is dark.

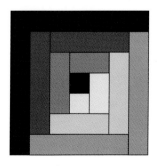

• Lay out the blocks in 7 rows of 6. Sew the blocks into rows and join the rows.
• Finish the quilt as described in *To Make a Quilt*, using the 2 1/2" x 44" red print strips for the binding.

Quilt-As-You-Sew Version of Straight Furrows

For this method, the materials for the quilt top are the same. For the backing, cut forty-two 16" squares of feedsack fabric. Also cut 1"-wide strips from approximately 3/4 yards of feedsack prints. Cut forty-two 16" squares of batting in place of the 89" x 103" piece of batting.
• Place a 16" feedsack square right side down on the work surface.
• Center a 16" square of batting on it.
• Place a 2 1/2" red print square, right side up, in the center of the batting square and pin in place.
• Lay a 2 1/2" light print square on top of the red square, right sides together, and stitch a 1/4" seam along the right edge of the fabrics, through all layers.
• Open the light print square and finger-press it away from the center. Pin the square in place.

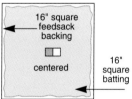

• Continue adding strips, as in the original directions, but sewing through all layers. Press the finished block carefully.
• Trim the backing even with the edges of the block. Trim the batting 1/4" inside the block edges on each side to reduce bulk.
• Lay out the blocks in 7 rows of 6. Place 2 blocks right sides together and pin them, keeping the backing out of the way. Stitching only through the top fabrics, sew the blocks together. Whipstitch the batting.
• Sew the blocks in pairs and then into rows. Use the same method to join the rows.
• To finish the back, turn under a 1/4" allowance on one side of each seam. Pin the folds together and whipstitch them. Turn under a 1/4" allowance on both sides of each 1"-wide strip. Appliqué a strip in place to cover each seam.
• Finish the quilt as described in *To Make a Quilt* using the nine 2 1/2" x 44" strips for binding.

▲ *Jeannette Fenner Knauff of Hillsboro, Ohio, set out to make a quilt with all feedsack fabrics, but didn't stop with just one.* **"Straight Furrows"** *(85" x 99") is her ninth Log Cabin variation, all inspired by a quilt shown in a 1980 issue of* Woman's Day. *Jeannette used a "quilt-as-you-sew" method, creating a patchwork back.*

Appalachian Sunset

Charming feedsack prints evoke warm memories of days gone by!

QUILT SIZE: 86" square
BLOCK SIZE: 12" square

MATERIALS

Yardage is estimated for 44" fabrics. We recommend making a sample block before cutting the fabric for the whole quilt. Please note that our instructions call for a traditional binding rather than the pieced prairie points shown in the photo. Tips for making the pieced prairie points are included if you'd like to try your hand at them.

- Assorted prints totaling at least 5 yards
- 5 yards muslin
- 1 yard blue
- 3/4 yard pale yellow print
- 3/4 yard multicolor print for the binding
- 7 3/4 yards backing fabric
- 90" square piece of batting

CUTTING

Pattern pieces are full size and include a 1/4" seam allowance, as do all dimensions given.

- Cut 588: A, assorted prints
- Cut 196: B, muslin
- Cut 196: C, muslin
- Cut 196: D, muslin
- Cut 196: E, blue; or cut ninety-eight 3 3/8" squares, then cut each in half diagonally to yield 196 triangles.
- Cut 49: F, pale yellow print
- Cut 8: 1 1/2" x 44" strips, muslin, for the border
- Cut 9: 2 1/2" x 44" strips, multicolor print, for the binding

DIRECTIONS

For each of the 49 blocks:

- Sew a print A to a muslin B to make Unit 1. Make 4.

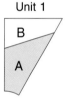
Unit 1

- Sew a print A and a blue E to opposite long sides of a muslin C to make Unit 2. Make 4.

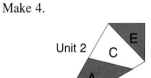
Unit 2

- Sew a print A to a muslin D to make Unit 3. Make 4.

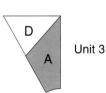
Unit 3

- Sew a Unit 1 and a Unit 3 to opposite sides of a Unit 2, as shown, to make a quarter-block. Make 4.

- Sew the 4 quarter-blocks together to make a block. It will have a hole in the center. Make 49.

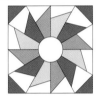

- Center a pale yellow F on a block. Pin it in place, making sure that the raw edges of the block center are covered. Baste the F in place.
- Appliqué the F to complete the block. Press. Make 49.
- Lay out the 49 blocks in 7 rows of 7. Sew the blocks into rows. Join the rows.
- Sew two 1 1/2" x 44" muslin strips together, end to end, to make a pieced border. Make 4. Sew 2 of them to opposite sides of the quilt. Trim the excess from the strips.
- Sew the remaining pieced borders to the remaining sides of the quilt. Trim as before.
- Finish the quilt as described in *To Make a Quilt*, using the 2 1/2" x 44" multicolor print strips for the binding.

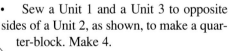

A

B

▶Paula Hammer's old-fashioned **"Appalachian Sunset"** (86" square) was made using 6" feedsack squares that she had traded and collected as a member of a Feedsack Club. Even the blue triangles at the corners of the blocks were made from solid blue feedsacks she had collected. Machine pieced and hand quilted with cotton batting, this quilt is a loving tribute to quilting's thrifty past. Even the batting was an exercise in thrift because Paula won it as a door prize!

Pieced Praire Points

Follow these directions to finish your quilt with novel pieced prairie points instead of a traditional binding. Use a wide assortment of scrap fabrics to cut the pattern pieces.

CUTTING
- Cut 96: G, assorted prints
- Cut 96: H, assorted prints
- Cut 48: J, backing fabric

DIRECTIONS
- Layer the backing, batting and quilt top as described in *To Make a Quilt*. Quilt as desired, leaving 1" around the outside unquilted.
- Sew a print G to a print H to make a pieced triangle. Make 96.

- Sew two pieced triangles together to make a pieced prairie point. Make 48.

- Sew a pieced prairie point to a backing print J, right sides together, sewing the short sides only. Turn the pieced prairie point right side out. Press. Make 48.

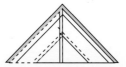

- Lay out the prairie points around the edges of the quilt, using 12 on each side. Place the pieced sides right side down on the quilt top with the points toward the center, overlapping them slightly. Align the raw edges of the prairie points with the raw edge of the quilt top. Keeping the backing free, pin the prairie points in place and sew them to the quilt top and batting with a 1/4" seam allowance.

- Turn the points away from the quilt and lightly press just the seam allowance to the wrong side. Trim the batting in the seam allowance to reduce bulk, if desired.
- Trim the backing 1/2" beyond the edge of the quilt top.
- Fold 1/2" of the backing to the wrong side and slipstitch the folded edges together to encase the seam allowances and complete the quilt.

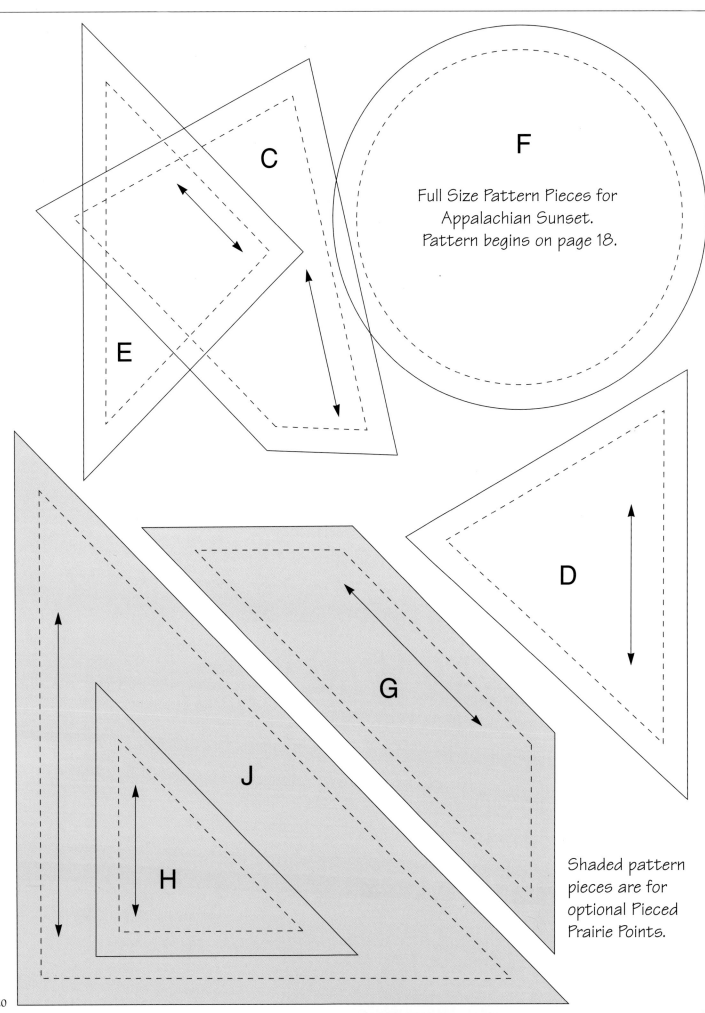

C

F

Full Size Pattern Pieces for
Appalachian Sunset.
Pattern begins on page 18.

E

D

G

J

H

Shaded pattern
pieces are for
optional Pieced
Prairie Points.

Dresden Plates

Dress up traditional blocks with triple sashing and a bright swag border.

QUILT SIZE: 104" square
BLOCK SIZE: 14"

MATERIALS
Yardage is estimated for 44" fabric.
- 1/4 yard light blue
- Assorted print scraps totaling approximately 4 yards
- 4 1/2 yards pink
- 7 3/4 yards white for background
- 9 1/4 yards backing fabric
- 108" square piece of batting

CUTTING
Pattern piece A is full size and includes a seam allowance. Appliqué pattern pieces B, C, D and E are full size and do not include a seam allowance. Make templates for each of the pattern pieces. Trace around the templates on the right side of the fabric and add 1/8" to 3/16" turn-under allowance when cutting the pieces out. All other dimensions include a 1/4" seam allowance. NOTE: Cut the lengthwise strips parallel to the selvage first, before cutting the smaller pieces from the same fabric.

(Continued on the following page)

▶*Paula Hammer of Lilburn, Georgia, brought the fabric she obtained in trades with her feedsack club to a mountain retreat with her "stitchin' group." That's where she made **"Dresden Plates"** (104" square). The grid-like pattern of the triple sashing and Nine Patch cornerstones act as a pleasing contrast to the circular Dresden Plate blocks and swag border.*

- Cut 400: A, assorted scraps
- Cut 25: B, light blue
- Cut 4: 8" x 107" lengthwise strips, white, for the border
- Cut 25: 14 1/2" squares, white
- Cut 15: 1 1/2" x 60" strips, white
- Cut 8: 1 1/2" x 44" strips, white
- Cut 11: 2 1/2" x 44" strips, white, for binding
- Cut 30: 1 1/2" x 60" strips, pink
- Cut 7: 1 1/2" x 44" strips, pink
- Cut 20: C, pink
- Cut 4: D, pink
- Cut 24: E, pink

PIECING

- Sew 16 A's together in pairs, starting at the narrow ends and stopping 1/4" from the wide ends and backstitching. Make 8 pairs.

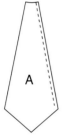

- Join the 8 pairs in the same manner to make a plate. Make 25.

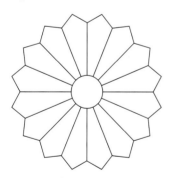

- Press the outside edge of each plate under 1/4". Center and pin each plate to a 14 1/2" white square. Appliqué in place.
- Center and pin a light blue B on each plate, covering the seam allowances. Appliqué each B in place, turning the edge under as you stitch. Set aside the 25 blocks.
- Sew a 1 1/2" x 44" pink strip and a 1 1/2" x 44" white strip together along their length to make a pieced strip. Make 5.
- Take 2 of these and sew a 1 1/2" x 44" pink strip to the white strip of each. In the same manner, sew a 1 1/2" x 44" white

strip to the pink strip of the 3 remaining pieced strips. Press the seam allowances in each pieced strip toward the pink.
- Cut enough 1 1/2" slices from each pieced strip to yield 72 slices with white on the outside and 36 with pink on the outside.

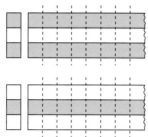

- Sew 3 of the slices into a Nine Patch with white squares in the four corners, as shown. Make 36.

- Sew a 1 1/2" x 60" white strip between two 1 1/2" x 60" pink strips along their length to make a pieced strip. Make 15.
- Cut four 14 1/2" slices from each pieced strip to yield 60 pieced sashing units.
- Lay out five blocks and 6 pieced sashing units as shown. Sew them into a row. Make 5.

- Lay out 5 sashing units and 6 Nine Patches, as shown. Sew them into a row. Make 6.

- Lay out the rows of blocks and the sashing rows, alternating them. Join them to complete the quilt center.
- Center and sew 8" x 107" white strips to opposite sides of the quilt center, starting and stopping 1/4" from the raw edges.
- Center and sew 8" x 107" white strips to the remaining sides of the quilt in the same manner. Miter each corner, referring to the mitering section in *To Make a Quilt*, as needed.
- Referring to the quilt photo, lightly mark the placement of the swags on the

border. Pin the C's along the sides and the D's in the corners and appliqué them in place. Appliqué the pink E's last.
- Finish the quilt as described in *To Make a Quilt*, using the 2 1/2" x 44" white strips for binding.

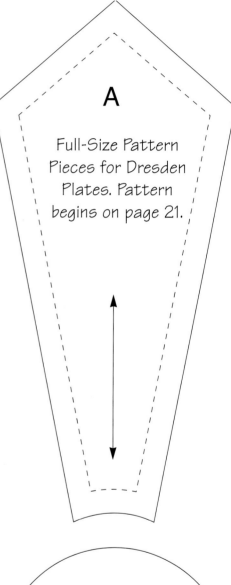

A

Full-Size Pattern Pieces for Dresden Plates. Pattern begins on page 21.

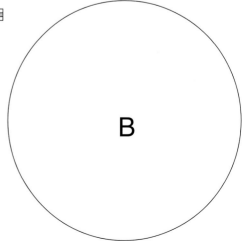

B

Full-Size Appliqué Pieces for
Dresden Plates Border.

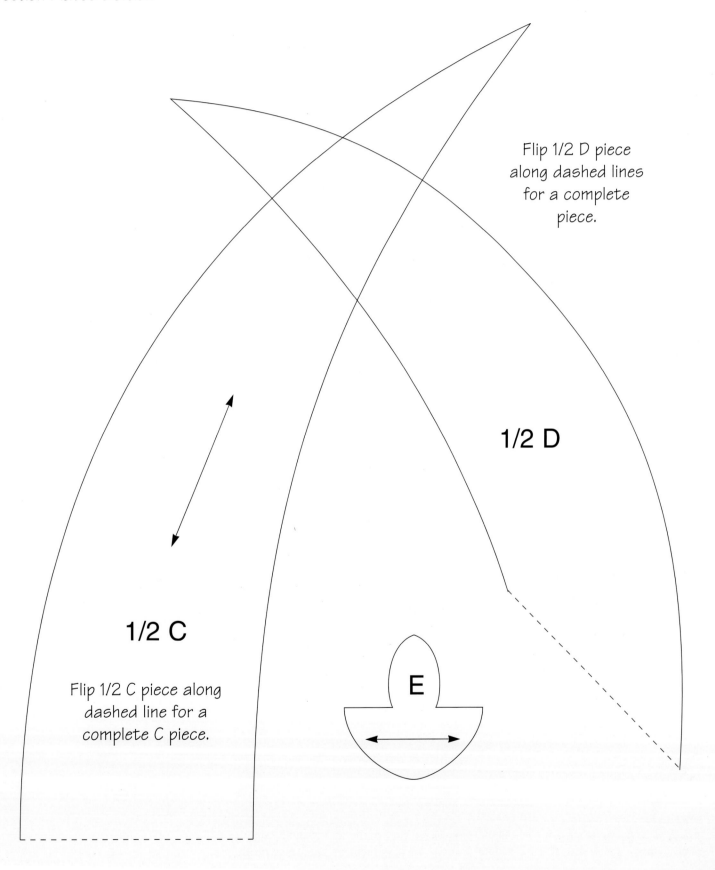

Flip 1/2 D piece
along dashed lines
for a complete
piece.

1/2 D

1/2 C

Flip 1/2 C piece along
dashed line for a
complete C piece.

E

Plaid Holes in the Barn Door

Use templates or rotary cut pieces for this classic.

QUILT SIZE: 65" x 79"
BLOCK SIZE: 6"

MATERIALS

Yardage is estimated for 44" fabric.
- 80 plaid scraps, each at least 6" square
- Assorted stripe scraps totaling 1 3/4 yards for the prairie points
- 4 yards muslin
- 2 1/4 yards pink print for cornerstones and border
- 4 yards backing fabric
- 69" x 83" piece of batting

CUTTING

Pattern pieces are full size and include a 1/4" seam allowance, as do all dimensions given. We recommend making a sample block before cutting fabric for the whole quilt. Cut lengthwise strips before cutting other pieces from that fabric.

From each 6" square plaid scrap:
- Cut 4: B; or cut four 1 1/2" x 2 1/2" strips
- Cut 4: A; or cut two 2 7/8" squares; then cut each in half diagonally

Also:
- Cut 80: C, muslin; or 2 1/2" squares
- Cut 320: A, muslin or cut one hundred and sixty 2 7/8" squares; then cut each in half diagonally
- Cut 320: B, muslin; or cut three hundred and twenty 1 1/2" x 2 1/2" strips
- Cut 178: 1 1/2" x 6 1/2" strips, muslin
- Cut 2: 3 1/2" x 73" lengthwise strips, pink print, for the borders
- Cut 2: 3 1/2" x 65" lengthwise strips, pink print, for the borders
- Cut 99: 1 1/2" squares, pink print for the cornerstones
- Cut 96: 5" squares, assorted stripes, for the prairie points

PIECING

For each of the 80 blocks:
- Sew a plaid A to a muslin A

to make a pieced square A. Make 4.
- Sew a plaid B to a muslin B to make a pieced square B. Make 4.

- Lay out the pieced squares and a muslin C, as shown. Sew the squares into rows, then join the rows to complete a block. Make 80.

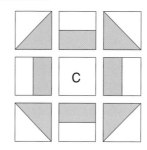

ASSEMBLY

- Referring to the photo, arrange the blocks in 10 horizontal rows of 8, leaving space between them for the sashing. Place a 1 1/2" x 6 1/2" muslin sashing strip between the blocks and at each end of each horizontal row.
- Stitch the blocks and sashing strips into rows. Press the seam allowances toward the sashing strips.
- Stitch nine 1 1/2" pink print cornerstones and eight 1 1/2" x 6 1/2" muslin sashing strips together into a long row, beginning and ending with the cornerstones. Press the seam allowances toward the sashing strips. Make 11.
- Join the rows of blocks and sashing rows, alternating them, beginning and ending with the sashing rows.
- Measure the length of the quilt. Trim the 3 1/2" x 73" pink print strips to equal that measurement. Sew them to the sides of the quilt.
- Measure the width of the quilt, including borders. Trim the 3 1/2" x 65" pink print strips to equal that measurement. Sew

them to the remaining sides of the quilt.
- Layer the backing, batting and quilt top as described in *To Make a Quilt*. Quilt as desired, leaving 1" around the outside unquilted.
- Fold a 5" square in half diagonally, wrong sides together. Then fold it in half again, forming a prairie point. Make 96.
- Lay out the prairie points around the edges of the quilt. Place the fold of each new point inside the opening of the last one, overlapping them as needed to make them fit. Use 22 each for the top and bottom edges and 26 for each side.
- Keeping the backing free, pin the prairie points to the quilt, aligning the raw edges of the prairie points with the edge of the quilt top and matching the triangles in the corners. The points will be toward the quilt center.
- Sew the prairie points to the quilt top and batting with a 1/4" seam allowance.
- Turn the points away from the quilt and lightly press just the seam allowance to the wrong side.
- Trim the backing 1/2" beyond the edge of the quilt top.
- Fold 1/2" of the backing to the wrong side and slip stitch the edges to encase the seam allowances and complete the quilt.

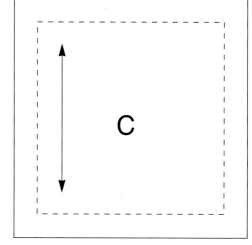

▶ *Paula Hammer created **"Plaid Holes in the Barn Door"** (65" x 79") as a result of trading 6" feedsack charm squares with friends and members of The Feedsack Club. She used plaids and stripes from her collection for the blocks and finished the edges with striped prairie points.*

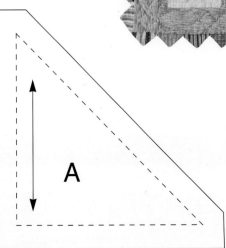

A

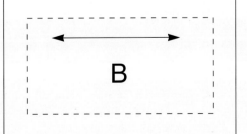

B

Full-Size Pattern Pieces for Plaid Holes in the Barn Door.

My Sunshine Quilt

Piece this classic using vintage or reproduction fabrics.

◄ *Inspired by an antique quilt, Ellie Hudacsek, stitched **"My Sunshine Quilt"** (69" x 80"). Ellie used muslin and old cotton feedsacks to achieve a '30's look. By alternating muslin blades with print ones, Ellie achieved the sun-ray effect.*

QUILT SIZE: 69" x 80"
BLOCK SIZE: 8"

MATERIALS

Yardage is estimated for 44" fabric.
• 72 scraps of light, medium and dark print fabrics, each at least 8" x 10", or scraps totaling 4 1/4 yards
• 3 3/4 yards muslin
NOTE: *This yardage includes enough fabric for you to appliqué the fans to a background square, if you prefer.*
• 1 yard red print
• 2/3 yard green print
• 4 yards backing fabric
• 73" x 84" piece of batting

CUTTING

Pattern pieces are full size and include a 1/4" seam allowance, as do all dimensions given. We recommend making a sample block before cutting pieces for the whole quilt.
For each of 72 Fan blocks:
Group the pieces for each block as you cut them.
• Cut 4: A, print
• Cut 1: B, same print
Also:
• Cut 216: A, muslin
• Cut 72: C, muslin
NOTE: *If you prefer to appliqué the fans, cut seventy-two 8 1/2" squares for the block background instead of the muslin C's.*
• Cut 6: 12 5/8" squares, red print; then cut each in quarters diagonally to yield 24 setting triangles. You will use 22.
• Cut 2: 6 5/8" squares, red print; then cut each in half diagonally to yield 4 corner triangles
• Cut 8: 2 1/2" x 44" strips, green print, for the binding

PIECING

For each of 72 blocks:
• Lay out 4 print A's and 3 muslin A's for one block.
• Sew a print A to a muslin A to make a pieced unit.

Full-Size Pattern Pieces for
My Sunshine Quilt.

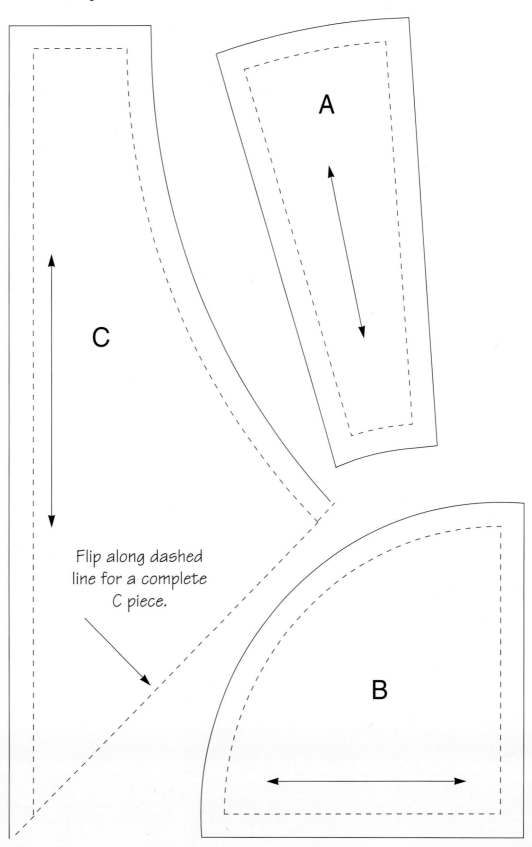

C

A

Flip along dashed
line for a complete
C piece.

B

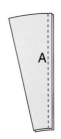

- In the same manner, join the remaining print and muslin A's to the pieced unit to make a Fan unit, as shown.

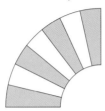

- Fold the fan unit in half to find the center. Make a small pencil mark at the mid-point on each curved edge as shown. Fold the matching print B in half to find the mid-point of the curved edge.

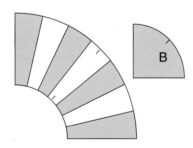

- Place the inside curved edge of the Fan unit on the curved edge of the print B, right sides together. Line up the pencil marks and pin. Align the curved raw edges, placing a pin at each end of the seamline.

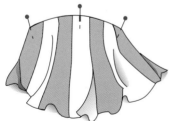

- Sew, manipulating the Fan unit to keep the raw edges aligned. Press the seam allowance toward the print B.
- In the same manner, mark, pin and sew a muslin C to the outside curved edge of the Fan unit. Press the seam allowance toward the fan to complete the block. Make 72. NOTE: *Appliqué each fan unit to an 8 1/2" square, if you prefer.*

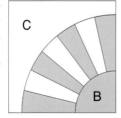

ASSEMBLY

- Referring to the photo, lay out the Fan blocks, setting triangles and corner triangles.
- Sew them into diagonal rows and join the rows.
- Finish the quilt as described in *To Make a Quilt*, using the 2 1/2" x 44" green print strips for the binding.

Railroad

String piecing means a random riot of color for this pieced favorite.

QUILT SIZE: 71" x 86"
BLOCK SIZE: 14"

MATERIALS
Yardage is estimated for 44" fabric.
- Assorted print scraps totaling at least 3 yards, for the blocks
- 29 print scraps each at least 6" square, for the pieced border
- 4 3/4 yards muslin
- 5 1/4 yards backing fabric
- 75" x 90" piece of batting

CUTTING
Dimensions include a 1/4" seam allowance.
NOTE: *Cut the lengthwise muslin border strips first, before cutting the smaller pieces from that fabric. You may wish to cut them an inch or two wider than specified to allow for variations in the quilt center and the pieced border. Trim the width of the muslin border strips to fit when the pieced border is ready to sew to the quilt.*
- Cut approximately 500: 3 1/2"-long strips, assorted prints, in random widths ranging from 1 1/4" to 2 1/2"
- Cut 29: 5 7/8" squares, assorted prints
NOTE: *These squares will be used to make pieced squares. If you have 6" square prints from an exchange, you can use them in that size, trimming them only after you sew the diagonal seams. In this case, you may wish to cut the following muslin squares the same size.*
- Cut 29: 5 7/8" squares, muslin
- Cut 80: 6" squares, muslin; then cut each in half diagonally to yield 160 triangles
- Cut 2: 2 1/2" x 74" lengthwise strips, muslin, for the border
- Cut 2: 3" x 64" lengthwise strips, muslin, for the border
- Cut 8: 2 1/2" x 44" strips, muslin, for binding

PIECING
- Randomly sew enough assorted print strips together along their 3 1/2" sides to make a pieced unit 11" long. Choose wider strips for the ends to prevent having seams close to the corner of the square. Make 80.
- Center and sew a muslin triangle to opposite sides of the pieced units, taking care not to stretch the bias edge of the triangle. Trim to make a 7 1/2" square. Make 80.
- Group the squares in sets of four, laying them out so that four muslin

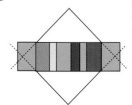

Glenda Henry, of Hartford, Kentucky, has collected a stack of over 500 different feedsack designs in the past eight years and she doesn't waste a scrap from any of them. Her string-pieced "Railroad" quilt (71" x 86") is great for using up those odd-sized pieces.

triangles form a square in the center. Pin and sew the squares together in pairs. Join the pairs to make a block. Make 20.

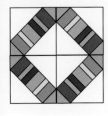

• Lay out 5 rows of 4 blocks. Sew the blocks into rows and join the rows.
• Measure the length of the quilt. Trim the 2 1/2" x 74" strips to that measurement and sew them to opposite sides of the quilt.
• Measure the width of the quilt. Trim the 3" x 64" strips to that measurement and sew them to the top and bottom of the quilt.
• Draw a diagonal line from corner to corner on the wrong side of each 5 7/8" muslin square.
• Lay a marked square on a 5 7/8" print square, right sides together, and sew 1/4" away from the diagonal line on both sides. Cut the squares apart on the

marked lines to yield 58 pieced squares. Open them and press the seam allowances toward the print.
• Referring to the quilt for placement, sew 15 pieced squares together to make a long side border. Make 2.
• In the same manner, make 2 short pieced rows with 14 pieced squares each.
• Sew the long pieced rows to the sides of the quilt. Sew the short pieced rows to the top and bottom of the quilt.
• Finish the quilt as described in *To Make a Quilt*, using the 2 1/2" x 44" muslin strips for binding.

Ohio Star

Patriotic pride shows in this traditional favorite.

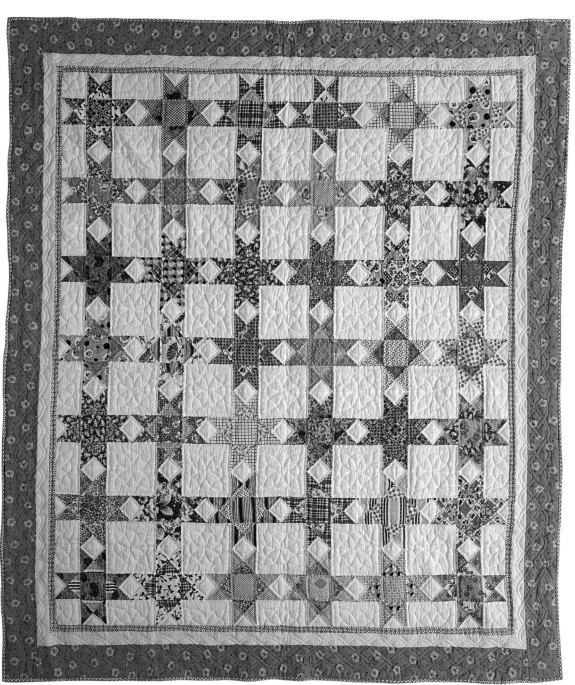

▲ *Paula Hammer lives in a suburb of Atlanta, Georgia, so it was only natural for her to use red, white and blue feedsack fabrics in* **"Ohio Star"** *(67" x 76"), her tribute to the 1996 Olympics. It's amazing how varied each Ohio Star looks—it's all in the printed fabric!*

QUILT SIZE: 67" x 76"
BLOCK SIZE: 9"

MATERIALS
Yardage is estimated for 44" fabric.
• Assorted red and blue scraps totaling at least 2 1/2 yards
• 2 1/4 yards blue print for the outer border
• 3/4 yard red print for the inner border and binding
• 3 yards white
• 4 1/2 yards backing fabric
• 71" x 80" piece of batting

CUTTING
Dimensions include a 1/4" seam allowance.
NOTE: *Cut the lengthwise white border strips first, before cutting any other pieces from that fabric.*
For each of 42 blocks:
Keep pieces for each block together as you cut them.
• Cut 1: 4 1/4" square, white
• Cut 1: 3 1/2" square, first red or blue print, for block center
• Cut 2: 4 1/4" squares, same red or blue print
• Cut 1: 4 1/4" square, second red or blue print

Also:

- Cut 168: 3 1/2" squares, white
- Cut 6: 1" x 44" strips, red print, for the inner border
- Cut 4: 2" x 68" strips, white, for the middle border
- Cut 4: 4 1/2" x 70" strips, blue print, for the outer border
- Cut 7: 2 1/2" x 44" strips, red print, for the binding

PIECING

For each block:

- Draw diagonal lines in both directions on the wrong side of the 4 1/4" white square and the 4 1/4" second red or blue print square.
- Lay a marked white square on one of the 4 1/4" first red or blue print squares, right sides together, and sew 1/4" away from one of the diagonal lines on both sides, as shown.
- Cut the squares apart on both drawn lines to yield four pieced triangles. Open the triangles and press the seam allowances toward the darker fabric.

- In the same manner, lay a marked second red or blue print square on the remaining 4 1/4" first red or blue print square, right sides together. Sew 1/4" away from one diagonal line on both sides, as before. Cut the square apart on the drawn lines to yield four pieced triangles. Open the triangles and press the seam allowances toward the darker fabric.
- Stitch one of each kind of pieced triangles into a pieced square. Make 4.
- Lay out these pieces for a block: 4 pieced squares, 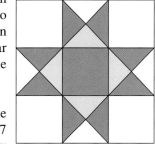 the 3 1/2" first red or blue print square and four 3 1/2" white squares. Sew them into rows and join the rows to complete an Ohio Star block. Make 42.

- Lay out the blocks in 7 rows of 6. Sew the blocks into rows and join the rows.

- Sew the six 1" x 44" red print strips together, end to end, to make a pieced strip for the inner border. Measure the length of the quilt. Cut two strips equal to that measurement from the pieced strip and sew them to opposite sides of the quilt.
- Measure the width of the quilt, including the borders. Cut two strips equal to that measurement from the pieced strip and sew them to the top and bottom of the quilt.
- Trim 2 of the 2" x 68" white strips to fit the quilt's length and sew them to opposite sides of the quilt.
- Trim the remaining two 2" x 68" white strips to fit the quilt's width and sew them to the top and bottom of the quilt.
- In the same manner, trim 2 of the 4 1/2" x 70" blue print strips to fit the quilt's length and sew them to opposite sides of the quilt. Trim the remaining 2 blue print strips to fit the quilt's width and sew them to the top and bottom of the quilt.
- Finish the quilt as described in *To Make a Quilt,* using the 2 1/2" x 44" red print strips for binding.

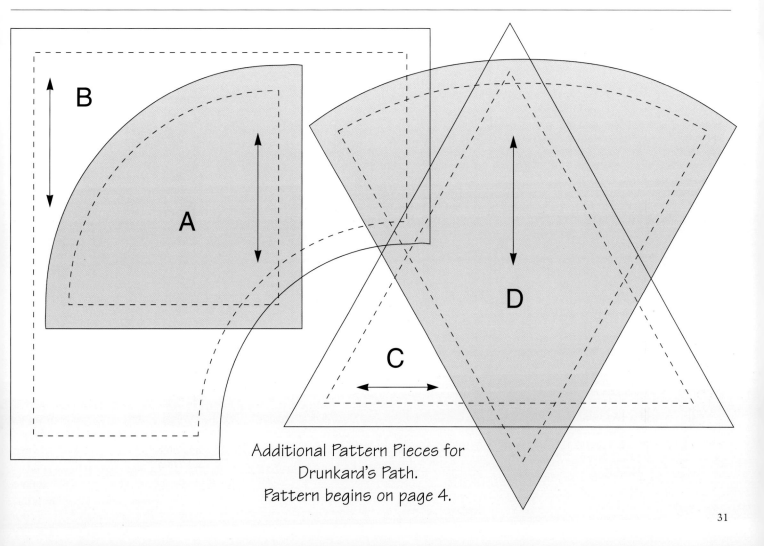

Additional Pattern Pieces for Drunkard's Path.
Pattern begins on page 4.

To Make A Quilt

CHOOSING A PATTERN

Read through all directions when choosing a pattern. The pattern pieces are full size. Unless otherwise noted, all pieces include 1/4" seam allowances. The solid line is the cutting line and the dashed line is the stitching line.

An "R" means that you will need to reverse that pattern piece before tracing.

FABRIC

Yardage requirements are based on 44"-wide fabric. Listed amounts are adequate, but little is allowed for errors. We suggest using 100% cotton fabrics.

TEMPLATES

Firm, clear plastic is best for making templates. Place a sheet of template plastic over the pattern pieces and accurately trace the cutting line and/or stitching line for each piece.

NOTE: Templates for machine piecing include a seam allowance. Templates for hand piecing usually do not. Templates for appliqué pieces usually do not include a seam allowance. Use a permanent marker to record on every template the name and size of the block, the grainline and the number of pieces needed for one block.

MARKING FABRICS

There are many marking tools available. Select the type you like best, remembering to test for removability. Keep these pointers in mind when marking: 1) If using pencil, sharpen it often. 2) Line up the grainline on the template accurately with the grainline of the fabric. 3) Place a piece of fine sandpaper under the fabric to prevent slipping. 4) For hand piecing, mark the wrong side of the fabric and flip all directional (asymmetrical) templates before tracing them. 5) Mark and cut just enough pattern pieces to make a sample block. Piece the block to determine the accuracy of each template. 6) Handle bias edges with care to avoid stretching.

When marking fabric for appliqué, trace the templates on the right side of the fabric, placing the wrong side of the template against the right side of the fabric. Leave at least 3/16" around hand appliqué templates to allow for a turn-under allowance on each piece. If using the buttonhole stitch or machine appliqué techniques, cut directly on the traced line.

PIECING

For machine piecing, set the stitch length at 12 stitches per inch and make sure the seamline lies exactly 1/4" from the edge of the fabric. Mark the throat plate with a piece of masking tape placed 1/4" away from the point at which the needle pierces the fabric. Unless otherwise noted, backstitching is not necessary for machine piecing. Start and stop stitching at the cut edges of the pieces. For set-in pieces, start and stop stitching 1/4" from the edges of the piece, backstitching at both ends.

When many of the same pieced unit are required, chain piece them through the machine without stopping. Leave the presser foot down and set the pieces against one another. Clip the threads after all the pieces are stitched.

When hand piecing, begin with a small backstitch. Continue stitching with a small running stitch, taking one small backstitch every 3 or 4 stitches. Stitch directly on the seamlines of each piece, from point to point, rather than from cut edge to cut edge. Finish each seam with another small backstitch.

APPLIQUÉ

To hand appliqué, baste or pin appliqué pieces to the background fabric. Turn the raw edges of each appliqué piece under with the tip of the needle and take small hidden stitches to secure the piece to the background.

To machine appliqué, baste pieces in place with a long machine basting stitch or a narrow, open zigzag stitch. Then stitch over the basting with a short, wide satin stitch. Placing a piece of paper between the wrong side of the fabric and the feed dogs of the sewing machine will help stabilize the fabric. Carefully remove excess paper when stitching is complete.

FINISHING
Pressing

Press seam allowances to one side unless otherwise directed. Press with a dry iron to avoid stretching fabric. Whenever possible, press seam allowances toward the darker of the two pieces. Otherwise, press toward the lighter fabric and trim away 1/16" from the darker seam allowance. This will prevent the darker fabric from showing through the top of the quilt. Press all blocks, sashings and borders before assembling the quilt top.

Mitering Corners

For mitered borders, the pattern allows extra length on each border strip. Stitch each border to the quilt top, beginning, and backstitching each seamline 1/4" from the edge of the quilt top. After all borders have been attached in this manner, miter one corner at a time. With the quilt top lying right side down, lay one border over the other. Draw a straight line at a 45° angle from the inner corner to the outer corner, as shown.

Reverse the positions of the borders and mark another straight line from corner to corner, in the same manner.

Place the borders, right sides together, with marked seamlines carefully matched and pinned and stitch from the outer to the inner corner backstitching at the inner corner. Open the mitered seam to make sure it lies flat, trim excess fabric and press.

Marking Quilting Lines

Mark the lines for quilting before basting the quilt together with the batting and backing. We suggest using a very hard (#3 or #4) pencil or a chalk pencil (for darker fabrics) though many marking tools are available. Test any marking method to be sure that the lines will wash out and not damage the fabric in any way. Transfer paper quilting designs by placing fabric over the design and tracing. A light box or a brightly lit window may be necessary when using darker fabrics. Precut plastic stencils allow you to trace the quilting design onto the fabric from the front. Check to be sure they fit the area you wish to quilt. Use a ruler to keep lines straight and even when marking grid lines.

Some quilting may be done without marking the top at all. Outline quilting (1/4" from the seamline) or quilting "in the ditch" can be done "by eye." Quilting "in the ditch" is done next to the seam (but not through it) on the patch opposite the pressed seam allowances.

Other straight lines may also be marked as you quilt by using the edge of masking tape as a stitching guide. For simple quilting motifs (hearts, stars, etc.) cut the shape(s) from clear, sticky-back paper (such as Contact® Paper) and position them on your quilt top. These shapes can be reused many times. Do not leave masking tape or adhesive paper on your quilt top overnight. Remove it when you are finished quilting for the day to avoid leaving a residue.

Basting

Cut the batting and backing at least 2" larger than the quilt top on all sides. Place the backing, wrong side up, on a flat surface and anchor in place with masking tape, if possible. Smooth the batting over the backing. Smooth the quilt top, right side up, over the batting. Baste the three layers together with thread or safety pins to form a quilt "sandwich." Beginning at the center of the quilt, baste horizontally first and then vertically. Add additional horizontal and vertical lines of stitches or pins approximately every 6" until the entire top is held together securely. Quilt as desired.

Binding

After the basting is removed, trim excess batting and backing to within 1/4" of the quilt top.

For most straight-edged quilts, a double-fold French binding is an attractive, durable and easy finish. NOTE: If your quilt has curved or scalloped edges, binding strips must be cut on the bias of the fabric. To make 1/2" finished binding, cut each strip 2 1/2" wide. Sew binding strips (cross grain or bias) together with diagonal seams; trim and press seams open.

Fold the binding strip in half lengthwise, wrong sides together, and press. Position the binding strip on the right side of the quilt top, aligning the raw edges of the binding with the edge of the quilt top, (not so that all raw edges are even.) Leave approximately 6" of binding strip free. Beginning several inches from one corner, stitch the binding to the quilt with a 1/2" seam allowance measuring from the raw edge of the backing. When you reach a corner, stop the stitching line exactly 1/2" from the edge. Backstitch, clip threads and remove the quilt from the machine. Fold the binding up and away, creating a 45° angle, as shown.

Keeping the angled folds secure, fold the binding back down. This fold should be even with the edge of the quilt top. Begin stitching at the fold.

Continue sewing the binding in this manner, stopping 6" from the starting point. To finish, fold both strips back along the edge of the quilt so that the folded edges meet about 3" from both lines of stitching and the binding lies flat on the quilt. Finger press to crease the folds. Cut both strips 1 1/4" from the folds.

Open both strips and place the ends at right angles to each other, right sides together. Fold the bulk of the quilt out of your way. Join the strips with a diagonal seam, as shown.

Trim the seam to 1/4" and press it open. Fold the joined strips so that wrong sides are together again. Place the binding flat against the quilt and finish stitching it to the quilt. Trim the layers as needed so that the binding edge will be filled with batting when you fold the binding to the back of the quilt. Blindstitch the binding to the back of the quilt, covering the seamline.

FINISHING THE QUILT

Remove any markings visible on the quilt top. Be sure to sign and date your quilt.